THE COLONIAL SOUTH

THE AMERICAN FOOD LIBRARY

A Guide to Regional Foods

THE COLONIAL SOUTH

written by
Anne Houlihan Brown

Rourke Publications, Inc.

The following sources are acknowledged and thanked for the use of their color transparencies in this work:
Georgia Department of Industry, Trade & Tourism pp. 20, 23; Janet Greenberg p. 7; Raymond J. Malace p. 33; North Carolina Division of Travel and Tourism pp. 2, 8, 15, 16, 21; Paul O'Connor pp. 35, 36, 40, 43; South Carolina Division of Tourism pp. 10, 14; Virginia Division of Tourism pp. 13, 18, 25, 26, 28, 29, 30, 46.
Cover photograph courtesy of Virginia Division of Tourism.
Food styling by David Hundley and Nancy Diamond.

Produced by Salem Press, Inc.

Copyright © 1994, by Rourke Publications, Inc.
All rights in this book are reserved. No part of this work may be used or reproduced in any manner whatsoever or transmitted in any form or by any means, electronic or mechanical, including any information storage and retrieval system, without written permission from the copyright owner except in the case of brief quotations embodied in critical articles and reviews. For information address the publisher, Rourke Publications, Inc., P.O. Box 3328, Vero Beach, Florida 32964.

∞ The paper used in this book conforms to the American National Standard for Permanence of Paper for Printed Library Materials, Z39.48-1984.

Library of Congress Cataloging-in-Publication Data
Brown, Anne H., 1953-
  The colonial South / by Anne H. Brown.
     p.   cm. — (The American food library)
  Includes index.
  ISBN 0-86625-509-5
  1. Cookery, American—Southern style—Juvenile literature. 2. Southern States—Description and travel—Juvenile literature. [1. Cookery, American—Southern style. 2. Southern States.] I. Title. II. Series.
TX715.2.S68B76   1994
641.5975—dc20   93-49008
                                                                    CIP
                                                                    AC

First Printing

PRINTED IN THE UNITED STATES OF AMERICA

Contents

1	An Introduction to the South	6
2	The Original Southerners	11
3	Southern Fairs and Pastimes	15
4	Agriculture in the South	19
5	Southern Customs	24
6	Regional Favorites	29
7	Breakfast in the South	34
8	Lunch in the South	36
9	Sunday Dinner	38
10	A Festive Barbecue Supper	42
	Glossary	47
	Index	48

1

AN INTRODUCTION TO THE SOUTH

Have you ever heard the term "southern hospitality," or talked to someone with a real "southern drawl?" Maybe you have a grandmother known for her "southern cooking." These are things we think of when we think of the South. But where is the South?

In the 1500s and the early 1600s, English, French, and Spanish colonists founded settlements along the Atlantic coast and on rivers in what are now Virginia, North Carolina, South Carolina, and northern Florida. As time passed and more Europeans came to the "New World," territories were settled all across the southern section of the country, stretching west into what is now Texas.

A farming economy emerged in the South and with it came the introduction of black Africans who were forced to work as slaves and servants. Many people in the North, and even some southerners, opposed the idea of slavery. In 1860-1861, eleven southern states seceded from the Union forming the Confederate States of America, or the Confederacy. Their hope was to establish a new country where this southern way of life could continue.

The divided United States of America fell into a civil war, North against South. When it ended in 1865, more than six hundred thousand men had died, and the defeated South was left in shambles.

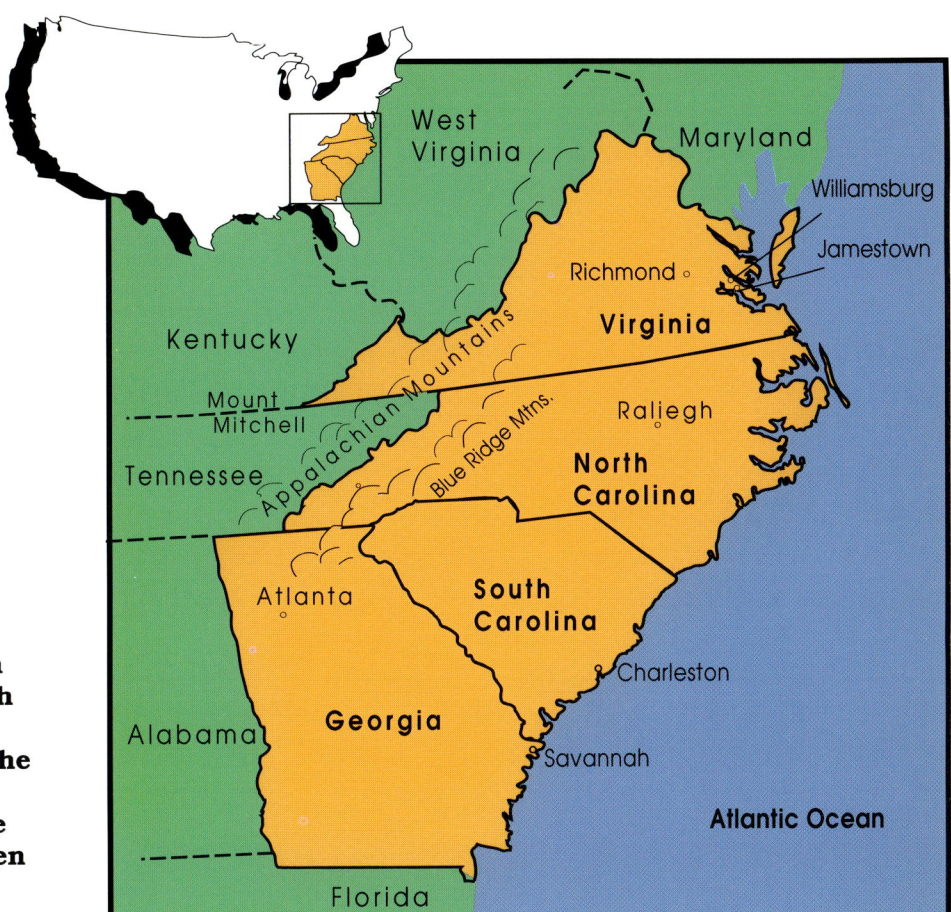

Virginia, North Carolina, South Carolina, and Georgia were the four southern Colonies of the original thirteen which became the U.S.A.

Entire cities—such as Richmond, Virginia, and Atlanta, Georgia—were in ruins. Countless homes and farmlands were destroyed. The war also left emotional and moral scars, which in various ways continue to shape a separate southern culture.

In the years since the Civil War, the South has grown to be many "Souths." Some areas remain agricultural and underdeveloped, others are growing centers of trade and business, still others draw tourists with their historical sights and mild climate. In our search for one of these Souths, we are going to concentrate on the Colonial South: Virginia, North Carolina, South Carolina, and Georgia.

The Land

This region is made up of two main geographic areas: the Coastal Plain and the Appalachian Mountains. The Coastal Plain varies in width from sixty-five to three hundred miles. In Virginia this area is known as the Tidewater; in North Carolina the chain of sandbars or barrier islands that run along the coast are called the Outer Banks; South Carolina's swampy coast is called the Low Country.

The Coastal Plain is level and sandy with an elevation nearly at sea level. Parts of this region lack good drainage and are marshy or boggy. On the border of Georgia and Florida is the Okefenokee Swamp. Moss-draped cypress trees and alligators dwell in this 650-square-mile wildlife refuge. On the border of Virginia and North Carolina is another wildlife preserve with a wonderful name: the Great Dismal Swamp.

Moving inland from the eastern shore, we find the Appalachian Mountains. This great mountain system extends from Newfoundland to Alabama and is older than the Rocky Mountains in the western

Harker's Island on North Carolina's Outer Banks is one of the many spots along the Atlantic coast where fishermen can set anchor.

United States. In North Carolina, Mount Mitchell rises to an elevation of 6,684 feet above sea level, making it the highest peak east of the Mississippi River.

These ancient mountains are forested with valuable timber, amounting to 40 percent of the nation's total commercial yield. The wood supplies the North Carolina furniture manufacturers, who ship their finished product all over the world. The Appalachians contain vast deposits of coal, iron, and other minerals.

Within the large Appalachian system there are individual mountain ranges. In Virginia, they are known as the Blue Ridge Mountains; in North Carolina, they are the Great Smokeys. Between the Appalachian chain and the Coastal Plain lies a band of rolling landscape known as the Piedmont. This hilly terrain is mainly agricultural and is bisected by many rivers which flow toward the Atlantic Ocean and the Gulf of Mexico.

The Towns

The earliest plantations and settlements in the South were located near the Atlantic Ocean and on rivers, which made it easier to transport both people and goods. Colonial Jamestown on the James River and Williamsburg between the James and the York Rivers were well located. The rivers served as a source of food and water power. They also provided a natural system of transportation in the days before roads were common.

The city of Charleston, founded in 1670, was originally the capital of South Carolina. Today, this historic city is one of the most important seaports on the Atlantic coast. Savannah, Georgia's oldest city, was founded in 1733 on the Savannah River near the Atlantic Ocean. Today it stands as a beautiful example of a planned city. Its symmetrical squares, parks, and broad avenues were fashioned after parts of seventeenth-century London. Atlanta, Georgia, is the largest city in the South. With a

population of five hundred thousand, it is nearly twice the size of any other southern town. More than twenty-two million people live in the states of Virginia, North Carolina, South Carolina, and Georgia. While this may seem like a huge number, it is far fewer than the nearly thirty million who live in California alone.

Southern life still takes place in small towns. The "county seat," with its fairs and social life, is an important gathering place for farmers and those living in rural areas. These people all see themselves as "southerners," but if you walk down the street in a typical small southern town, you might notice more differences than similarities in the people you meet. What is it that all of these people have in common? Let's look at three early groups: the Native Americans, the colonists, and the African slave population. We will see how their shared history helped shape the South as we know it today.

The true South can still be discovered in small-town life. Visitors to South Carolina might be lucky enough to join in a historic Spring Jubilee.

2

THE ORIGINAL SOUTHERNERS

For thousands of years, and long before there was a United States, the Southeast was home to tribes of Native Americans. Cherokee, Chickasaw, Seminole, Creek, Choctaw, and many other tribes lived in permanent villages throughout the South. Their way of life was based on a cooperation of efforts. The men hunted and the women raised the crops.

The first white colonists who came from England were lucky these Indians were there. Without their help, and their knowledge of food gathering and farming, those settlers might all have starved, not to mention that we would not have been introduced to corn and might be sitting through movies without any popcorn!

The Indians appreciated the fertility of this part of the country. There were at least fourteen thousand Native Americans living on the Virginia coast when the English arrived in 1607. In fact, the Indian name for the area meant "densely populated land."

The first permanent English settlement was Jamestown, named after the English king, James I. This first group of colonists was made up entirely of men. Led by Captain John Smith, they came to North America with the mistaken idea that they would find great stores of gold and silver as the Spanish had in Central and South America.

Although they brought with them seeds and cuttings of English fruits and vegetables, their early harvests were a disaster. These men had been tradesmen at home in England. They were not English gentlemen, who would have known how to shoot, hunt, and fish. Instead, the colonists spent most of their days panning for gold and quickly went through their provisions.

By observing the Indians and trading what they could, the colonists survived and learned to plant and hunt. Instead of gold, it was tobacco—a crop raised by the Indians—that finally brought financial success. Planting an imported West Indian seed in the fertile Virginia soil produced a leaf superior to the tobacco the Indians raised. Soon there was a demand from England for this tobacco, and for a time it was even used as legal tender, or money.

As more and more tobacco patches appeared along the James River, it became obvious that laborers were needed to tend this new and successful crop. In 1619, only twelve years after the settlement of Jamestown, a Dutch trade ship arrived carrying the first African slaves. Perhaps as many as fifteen slaves arrived on that original voyage. Very quickly, and for the next 150 years, slavery made possible the success of the southern plantation economy.

Further to the south in Charleston, South Carolina, or Charles Town as it was known in the late 1600s, another crop was introduced which added to the need for slave labor: rice. This grain flourished in the Low Country. Since rice grows standing in water, working conditions in the rice fields were hot, humid, and intolerable. Once again slavery was the only answer in the minds of the plantation owners.

By 1715, fifty thousand African men and women had been brought to Virginia and the Carolinas. In 1860, on the eve of the Civil War, there were four million black people living as slaves in the United States. Cotton, sugarcane, and indigo had been added to the list of southern slave crops. Besides working in the fields, many thousands more worked as footmen, personal servants, maids, and cooks.

When you visit Jamestown, the first permanent English settlement in the New World, you can observe modern-day "settlers" preparing a one-pot meal over an open fire.

The People of the South Today

Out of the hundreds of tribes of southeastern Indians, very few survived their interaction with the newcomers. Diseases brought by the Europeans and by the African slaves virtually wiped out the native people and with them much of their language and culture. There is a tribe of Lumbee/Cherokee Indians in North Carolina numbering some forty thousand people, and a small group of Catawba Indians still lives on a reservation in South Carolina. But for the most part, the native people were either displaced or died out in this part of the Southeast.

While the majority of southerners today are descendants of the British colonists—including the Scots and Irish—or the African slaves, there are people from all countries of the world in the South. Larger populations of Spanish are found in Florida, and in Louisiana the French influence is strong.

Hampton Plantation in South Carolina is one of the many stately homes which once housed the wealthy southern plantation owners.

3

SOUTHERN FAIRS AND PASTIMES

The North Carolina State Fair in Raleigh gives many children their first introduction to the state capital.

Fairs and festivals have long been part of southern life and leisure. Since the 1800s, agricultural fairs offered southern farmers an opportunity to view the newest innovative farm machinery and improved breeds of livestock. Often the location of the state fair gave rural children their first chance to see their state capital or larger cities.

Today's state and county fairs continue this tradition. Young farm children exhibit their prize cattle, sheep, and hogs. Award winning pies, jams, and farm produce usually are exhibited in nearby tents. A carnival midway is always part of the excitement with scary amusement rides and booths selling such "fair food" as hot dogs and cotton candy.

Typical of the small fairs held annually throughout the South is the Calvary, Georgia, Mule Day

The Apple Chill Festival in Chapel Hill, North Carolina is typical of the many southern festivals which celebrate local customs.

Festival in November. Here the mule is honored with a parade, followed by barrel racing, mule team pulling matches, and even a mule beauty contest! Local cooks sell barbecue, fried fish, and cane syrup made by a mule-driven sugarcane grinder. A good team of mules was an invaluable possession in earlier times. Mules were used to build river levees, clear forests, build roads, and plow fields. Mule breeding and raising is mainly done as a hobby these days, although the use of mules in the field is far from uncommon on small farms in the rural South.

Small town fairs serve to pass on traditions and customs with many themes. Buford, Georgia, has an annual Invitation Clog Dancing Hoedown, preserving a dance that originated with the Scots and the Irish. If there is a crop that grows or a fruit that is picked, there is a fair to honor it. South Carolina's oldest festival is the Hampton County Watermelon Festival, held annually since 1939. In St. George, South Carolina, they hold the World Grits Festival, and in Salley, they pay homage to "chitlins" at the Salley Chitlin Strut.

The Shenandoah Mountains of Virginia are covered with apple orchards thanks to George Washington, who required each of his tenants to plant four acres of trees. Each May when the trees are in bloom, the Shenandoah Apple Blossom Festival is held, and in September it's the Apple Harvest Festival in Winchester, Virginia.

One of the more sophisticated festivals in the South is the famous Spoleto Festival held in Charleston, South Carolina. As the American counterpart to the "sister" event held in Spoleto, Italy, this multi-dimensional affair presents more than one hundred performances and events in dance, theater, music, and art. A strong emphasis on education brings more than eight hundred young musicians to Spoleto to compete for the opportunity to join the Festival Orchestra and to travel to Italy at the close of the Charleston program.

Music has always played an important role in southern life. Family reunions, barn raisings, corn shuckings, and religious revivals gave regular folks an opportunity to "lay aside the plow and pick up the fiddle." Since the early 1900s, music festivals have grown in popularity. Fiddler's conventions, such as the ones held in Union Grove, North Carolina, Galax, Virginia, and around Asheville, North Carolina, draw thousands from all parts of the United States.

Southerners also love to gather in the name of sports, particularly at basketball and football games. There are usually fierce rivalries between small town teams, and the Friday night game—with its pep rallies and band performance—is not to be missed. In the predominately rural South, football and basketball teams foster a strong sense of community from town to town and from state to state.

The Old Fiddlers Convention in Galax, Virginia, gives music lovers a chance to show off their skills.

4

AGRICULTURE IN THE SOUTH

The southern climate and soil are perfectly suited for growing things. The sandy loam soil of the Coastal Plain is rich and easily cultivated. The farm lands of the Piedmont are fairly fertile too, but the Appalachian highlands have soils that tend to be thin and rocky.

Depending on the elevation, temperatures throughout this area remain fairly mild in the winter, rarely falling below freezing except in the mountains of North Carolina and Virginia. Long, humid summers in the Coastal Plain make it possible to grow crops as long as ten months a year.

Native Foods

Of all the contributions made to southern culture by the Native Americans, the most important may have been in agriculture. They raised squash, beans, peas, sweet potatoes, and onions, but by far the most versatile crop they grew was corn.

Maize, as the Indians knew it, was developed over a period of twenty-five hundred years from a wild grass that originally grew in the highlands of Mexico. That grass had an "ear" only one inch long with four rows of tiny kernels. Corn is the basis for many favorite southern dishes today: hominy, cornbread, hoecakes, spoonbread, grits, and corn pudding.

With a mild climate and rich soil, the list of native foods growing before the Europeans arrived was extensive. The Indians gathered nuts from hickory

and pecan trees. Wild strawberries, blackberries, blueberries, persimmon, and scuppernong grapes grew in abundance. Fruit trees yielded plums and cherries.

The Indians hunted all kinds of game: wild turkey, quail, duck, wild pig, deer, squirrel, opossum, and rabbit. They harvested 250 different kinds of fish and shellfish along the bays and inlets of the Atlantic coast. The fertile rivers were a source of bass, trout, catfish, and turtles.

The Native Americans gathered pecans from the trees that naturally grew in the South. Today, farmers grow them in orchards and harvest the crop. These orchards are in Georgia.

Foods of the Newcomers

Along with the British passengers making the crossing to the colonies in the early 1600s were a number of domestic animals. The colonists brought English shorthorn cattle, milk goats, sheep, chickens, and pigs. With plenty of corn to feed the pigs, pork quickly became a staple food of colonial life.

Pork and corn are still very basic to southern cooking. From these animals, milk, butter, and eggs were added to round out the colonial diet, along with the vegetables, fruits, and grains that were common in England. They also brought honey bees, which the Indians called "white man's flies."

More new foods came on the slave ships from Africa. Black-eyed peas, okra, watermelon, sweet potatoes, and peanuts arrived in this manner. The slaves brought a style of cooking that made use of spices and peppers unknown to the colonists and Indians.

Today

Some, but not all, of the crops grown in the Colonial South continue to be important today. The town of Charleston owed its colonial splendor to the success of the rice crops. With the end of slavery and

Southern farmers continue to harvest a wide variety of fresh vegetables and fruits. At the Farmers Market in Raleigh, North Carolina, you can buy direct from the source.

forced labor, it proved impossible to successfully mechanize this swampland crop. Production of rice moved to higher ground in Arkansas and Texas.

Corn, which sustained the Indians and settlers, is now grown as a feed grain and ranks among the top four cash crops in the states we are exploring. "Sweet corn" for eating is grown on small farms and in home gardens. Corn is also grown for use in the manufacture of methanol, a gasoline alternative.

Cotton, which was the major crop in Georgia for more than one hundred years, now amounts to just 2 percent of the farm income in that state. Its importance in the South has diminished with the growing competition from western states and other countries as well as with the development of synthetic fibers. Georgia now grows more peanuts and pecans than any other crop.

Tobacco was the crop that turned the tides for the desperate Jamestown settlers. While tobacco is a very labor intensive crop, requiring much handwork, it continues to be important. Although many Americans have stopped smoking tobacco, its use is growing in other parts of the world. Tobacco and tobacco processing are big business in the South.

Sharecropping

After the Civil War, most owners of large plantations were left with very little money to spend on laborers. Former slaves and landless whites were taken on as sharecroppers, or tenants. Under this arrangement, they were allowed to farm someone else's land in exchange for what was often an unfair share of the profits.

This system was responsible for the continued poverty that lasted into the 1940s, when tractors and cotton-picking machinery came into common use. Modernization forced many families to the cities

Peanuts are a major crop in Georgia. One half of the harvest is made into peanut butter.

in search of work or out of the South entirely.

In much of the South, poor farming practices over many generations depleted the soil. Where tobacco and cotton were "king," we now find soybeans, peanuts, peaches, pecans, and other crops.

5

SOUTHERN CUSTOMS

In the rural South, where people have always been close to the soil, it is natural that customs would develop around food, cooking, and eating. Many southerners were farmers and as such their principal occupation was growing food. Others raised a vegetable garden to supplement the needs of the kitchen. This was mainly the case in the years before World War II, before the arrival of big supermarkets and sophisticated farm machinery.

Families tended to be larger then, with five, seven, or more to feed, and grandparents or other relatives often lived close by. Work in the fields began after an early breakfast, and kitchen chores such as canning and preserving went on throughout the long day.

The big meal of the day was at noon. Southerners called this meal "dinner," not lunch. On most days, but especially Sundays, it was quite a big spread. The family table typically would hold fried chicken or roast pork with mashed potatoes or rice and gravy. There was lots of cornbread, green beans with bacon, yellow squash, sweet potatoes, and sliced tomatoes with cucumbers and onion. There was always fresh milk or buttermilk to drink, and lots of iced tea with homemade pies and cobblers for dessert.

"Southern hospitality" may be an overused term, but the love of cooking and entertaining is rooted in southern history. In the years of poverty following the Civil War, and again during the Great Depression, a tradition of southern hospitality was born out

Cooks at the American Frontier Culture Museum in Virginia still prepare food the old-fashioned southern way.

of great need and hunger. In these hard times, people would come together at the dinner table to share what they had with those who had less.

Food traditions also developed around the church, where large numbers gathered for a church supper and "dinner on the grounds." It also was customary for the preacher to be invited to Sunday dinner at the home of one of his parishioners. When there was a death, it was customary to bring a dish to the mourning family and fill the house with food and friends.

The South is a more modern place now, and with change food traditions have faded. With mothers and fathers working, few families have time to garden or cook large meals. The classic southern diet relies heavily on butter, eggs, sugar, and frying with oil or lard. This type of diet is looked upon as unhealthy today, although there is no reason to stop cooking and enjoying these delicious foods in moderation.

Southern Specialties

There are certain foods that we identify with the South, whether they originated with the Indians, the

Corn is a staple of Southern cooking. The original settlers learned to plant and grow it from the Indians. Here, children learn how to shuck corn.

European colonists, the Africans, or a combination of the three. Let's look at a few southern specialties and the history behind them.

Most people would agree that the South's most famous dish is fried chicken. Whether it is called Maryland fried, Kentucky fried, or southern fried, it is all delicious. Recipes for fried chicken have been turning up in southern cookbooks for more than 150 years. Wonderful both hot and cold, fried chicken is a favorite for picnics, holidays, and outdoor get-togethers.

Corn tops the list of important ingredients in southern cooking. Cornbread—made with ground cornmeal—is best when baked in a heavy iron skillet, sometimes in the shape of ears of corn. The earliest "cornbread" was cooked over a fire on a metal implement and called a hoecake or ash cake. Two other famous corn dishes are spoonbread and corn pudding, rich soufflé type recipes that have come down to us from a dish called Indian porridge. If you are not from the South, there is little chance that you have eaten grits. Grits are made from coarsely ground hard corn and are typically served boiled as part of breakfast. Don't give up on grits until you have had baked cheese-grits casserole.

Peanuts are a major crop in Georgia and one half of this crop is made into peanut butter. In the early days, farmers allowed their hogs to forage in the harvested peanut fields. A very distinctive ham was developed from these peanut-fed hogs. Smithfield hams, originating in Smithfield, Virginia, are famous the world over. Ten million hams are shipped out of this small town every year. The peanut diet of the hogs gives the ham a rich color and fine texture. These hams are cured, smoked, and aged in a process that can take from nine to twenty-one months. Similar "country" or "old" hams, are cured in other parts of the South. A slice of "old ham" served on a "beaten biscuit" is a very southern hors d'oeuvre, or appetizer.

The list of foods that southerners enjoy, and that non-southerners might not touch, goes on and on. Pickled okra, pickled pig's feet, chow-chow, watermelon rind pickles, and muscadine jam are condiments that are routinely "put-up" in southern kitchens. Breads such as beaten biscuits, salt-rising bread, buttermilk biscuits, cornpone, and hushpuppies are typically southern. Other dishes include catfish, frog legs, crowder peas, turnip greens, hoppin' John, stewed tomatoes, fried green tomatoes, black-eyed peas, and ambrosia. Wonderful southern desserts include pecan pie, chess pie, Jefferson Davis pie, sweet potato pie, divinity, and bourbon balls. Good southern cooks of all races and circumstances learned to take what the land would yield and turn it into something marvelous.

Smithfield Hams are famous for their rich flavor and fine texture. They are cured, smoked, and aged in a process that can take from nine to twenty-one months.

6

REGIONAL FAVORITES

While we have looked at foods that are popular across the South and dishes known to be especially "southern," there are also regional specialties. In certain parts of the South, people have special favorites, dishes made with foods found only in that area or foods passed down through a history unique to a certain group.

Along the coast and rivers, where the plantation

The Eastville Inn in Eastville, Virginia, offers visitors a delicious mixed seafood platter.

economy flourished, we find many recipes that make use of seafood. Around Charleston, they relish their she-crab soup, which gets its special flavor from the roe, or eggs, of the female crab. Crab imperial and deviled crab dishes are also common along the southern coast. From Virginia to Georgia, friends gather for oyster roasts in the months with an "R". Since oysters spawn from May to August, some states have laws against harvests during the summer months, the four months spelled without an "R."

In the Carolinas where rice was once a plantation crop, there are dozens of recipes called "pilaus." Spelled pilau, pilaf, perlew, or purloo, all are rice dishes with seafood, chicken, tomatoes, okra, or a variety of other ingredients. There is a similar dish favored in Georgia called Country Captain, made with chicken, currants, and rice.

Foods of the Planters

The plantation era was a time when much emphasis was placed on the fine art of entertaining. With large numbers of slaves to do the kitchen work, the planter's wife was free to plan elaborate meals. The ability to entertain lavishly became the hallmark of a great plantation house. Sumptuous dinners of Virginia ham, saddle of mutton, canvas back duck, beef, and oysters greeted many a visitor. Thomas Jefferson, the third President of the United States, was one of these wealthy Virginia plantation owners. While he was the American Ambassador to France, Jefferson went to great expense to bring one of his slaves to Paris to be trained by a French chef. He later gave this man, James Hemings, his freedom, but only with the promise that he would pass along his skills to his successor.

The heritage of "fancy" southern foods handed down in handwritten cookbooks from generation to generation is due in large part to the slave cooks who worked in the plantation kitchens. Working under desolate circumstances, they helped create the recipes

Plantations still represent some of the grandest homes in the Colonial South and reflect the best of early Southern architecture. Shirley Plantation, Charles City, Virginia.

for which southern cooking is best known today. At the same time, however, a separate style of cooking evolved, distinctly different from the English style of cooking preferred by the white planters.

Barbecue

The tradition of the barbecue dinner is found in all southern states. Its history goes back to the Caribbean Indians who were found cooking over open fires by the Spanish explorers. American Indians were also cooking in pits when the Europeans arrived, and by the end of the 1600s, there were laws in Virginia prohibiting the shooting of firearms at barbecues.

The word barbecue comes from the Spanish *barbacoa*, which described the wooden framework that held the meat over the firepit. In the Old South, barbecue pits were traditionally tended by black men who worked laboriously for eight to twelve hours basting whole pigs over slow burning coals of hickory wood. Most "pits" today are built above ground of block or brick, but barbecue is still a "slow food."

A barbecue is always a social event, and most southern communities have their local expert, or pit master, and their own special recipes. The meat, usually pork, can be minced, chopped, sliced, served on a bun or a plate with sauces that range from sweet to hot and tangy.

Debates over the best method of barbecuing and the best cuts of meat to use are fiercely regional. More important, barbecue dinners are a coming together of friends and neighbors at church suppers, political rallies, family reunions, or a simple backyard cookout.

Southern Soul Food

For the most part, slaves had to "make do" when it came time to feed their own families. They used what was available, relying on a variety of vegetable leaves, or "greens," bits and pieces of pork, an occasional chicken, lots of corn and cornmeal, and peppers and spices brought from Africa. In the 1960s the term "soul food" came to describe a whole range of African American recipes that need no label to those who grew up on them.

In this ingenious style of cooking, every conceivable part of the hog is used. Chitterlings, or "chitlins," is a dish made from the intestines. Pig's feet are pickled and roasted in a vinegar and brown sugar gravy. Hog jowl, or cheek, is cooked with black-eyed peas, an African import. "Greens"—turnip tops, collards, mustard greens, dandelion leaves, kale, or chard—are cooked with ham hocks. Okra, also brought from Africa, is stewed with tomatoes, corn, and bacon. Fried chicken and catfish with hush puppies are also standard fare.

The history of the South is reflected in the foods we cook and in the recipes that we will hand down. If you have a friend or grandparent who loves to cook, ask if you can help and learn a little bit about your own family history.

Some typical examples of soul food include (clockwise from bottom): barbequed ribs, black-eyed peas, greens with ham hocks, fried chicken, and cornbread.

Breakfast in the South

Fried Ham and Apples
Buttermilk Biscuits

Fried Ham and Apples

1 piece of center cut ham, $\frac{1}{2}''$ thick
3 tablespoons margarine
6 or 8 firm apples
2 or 3 pinches of brown sugar

1. Melt one tablespoon of margarine in a heavy iron skillet.
2. Cut the ham into 4 serving-size pieces and brown on both sides in the skillet over medium-high heat. Remove to a warm plate in a warm oven.
3. Add 2 more tablespoons of margarine to the skillet, scraping up any bits of ham from the bottom of the skillet with a spatula.
4. Core the apples, leaving the skins on, and cut them into $\frac{1}{2}''$ wedges.
5. Add the apples to the skillet, cover, and cook, stirring occasionally, until soft.
6. Toward the end of the cooking, remove the cover and add 2 or 3 pinches of brown sugar.
7. Pour any juice that accumulates over the ham.

Buttermilk Biscuits

2 cups all-purpose flour
3 teaspoons baking powder
6 tablespoons solid shortening
$\frac{1}{2}$ teaspoon baking soda
$\frac{1}{2}$ teaspoon salt
$\frac{2}{3}$ cup buttermilk

Note: Each recipe serves four, unless otherwise stated.

Fried Ham with Apples

1. Preheat the oven to 400 degrees
2. Sift together the dry ingredients.
3. With a fork, or your fingers, mix the shortening into the flour mixture until it resembles coarse meal.
4. Pour the buttermilk in very slowly, mixing with a fork until it will form a ball.
5. Shape it into a ball and roll it out on a floured board until it is $1/2''$ thick.
6. Cut out the biscuits using a biscuit cutter (or a small juice glass) and place the biscuits, just touching, on a lightly greased baking sheet.
7. Bake for 8 to 10 minutes, or until just browned. Serve with honey or jam and butter.

Lunch in the South

Crab Chowder
Skillet Cornbread

Crab Chowder

   5 tablespoons butter
   5 tablespoons flour
   2 cups chicken stock
   2½ cups half and half
   ⅓ cup finely chopped onion
   1½ cups corn (fresh cooked if possible)
   6 oz. crab meat
   salt and pepper to taste

Crab Chowder with Corn

1. Melt the butter in a heavy saucepan over low heat.
2. Add the flour, stirring quickly with a wire whisk until smooth.
3. Slowly add the chicken stock and then the half and half, stirring constantly with the whisk. Continue to cook over a very low flame for about 10 minutes, stirring frequently.
4. In a separate pan, sauté the onion in a little butter until transparent. Add the corn and crab and stir to mix.
5. Add this to the saucepan and cook for another 5 minutes. Season with salt and pepper.

Skillet Cornbread

3 beaten eggs
1 small carton of sour cream
½ cup vegetable oil
1 cup self-rising corn meal
1 cup canned cream-style corn

1. Place the greased iron skillet in a 400 degree oven.
2. Mix the eggs, sour cream, and oil in a mixing bowl.
3. Add the corn meal and corn and stir well.
4. Carefully pour into the hot skillet and bake for 20-30 minutes. Cut into wedges and serve with butter while hot.

Sunday Dinner

Oven Fried Chicken
Green Beans
Corn Pudding
Cucumbers and Onions with Sliced Tomatoes
Minted Iced Tea

Oven Fried Chicken

1 cut up chicken
1 cup all purpose flour
1 cup seasoned bread crumbs
2 eggs
1/3 cup buttermilk
salt and pepper
4 tablespoons butter

1. Preheat the oven to 350 degrees. Pat the chicken dry with paper towel.
2. In a shallow mixing bowl, beat the two eggs and add the buttermilk. Stir well.
3. In another bowl, combine the flour and crumbs and about ½ teaspoon each of salt and pepper.
4. Line a shallow roasting pan with foil to make clean up easier.
5. Dip the chicken in the egg mixture, one piece at a time. Coat well, then roll in the flour mixture, and shake off the excess. Place the chicken pieces in the roasting pan and carefully drizzle with melted butter.
6. Bake until browned, 50 to 60 minutes.

Green Beans

In the South, a "mess" of beans is cooked a long time until the beans are very tender.

2 pounds of fresh green beans
1 small piece of ham hock or 4 pieces of bacon, chopped
1 medium onion, chopped
2 tablespoons butter
1 teaspoon Worcestershire sauce
½ teaspoon sugar
1 teaspoon each salt and pepper

1. Melt the butter in a large sauce pan.
2. Cook the onion and ham hock over high heat for 5 minutes.
3. Add the green beans, washed, stringed, and snapped, and the rest of the ingredients.
4. Add enough water to cover, and simmer covered for 3 to 4 hours over low heat. Add water as necessary to keep from drying out. Serves four with leftovers.

Corn Pudding

(This is a vegetable dish, not a dessert.)

4 cups cream-style corn *
⅓ cup sugar mixed with
2 tablespoons of flour
1 teaspoon salt
½ teaspoon white pepper
2 cups of milk
4 beaten eggs
1 tablespoon melted butter

1. Put the corn in a large mixing bowl. Add the sugar and flour and mix.
2. Add the milk, eggs, butter and stir well.
3. Pour into a $2\frac{1}{2}$ quart Pyrex casserole dish.
4. Place the dish inside a larger pan and put in the oven.
5. Add $1\frac{1}{2}$ inches of water to the outer pan and bake at 325 degrees for 1 hour and 20 minutes, or until set.

* Fresh corn, cut and scraped from the cob, is best. You will need about 8 ears. Canned cream-style can be used.

Cucumber and Onions with Sliced Tomatoes

Cucumber and Onions with Sliced Tomatoes

1 peeled cucumber, cut in ¼" slices
2 small sweet yellow onions, cut in ¼" slices
3 cups cold water
1 cup white vinegar
1 teaspoon salt
1 teaspoon sugar
½ teaspoon dill
2 large tomatoes

1. Put the water, vinegar, salt, sugar, and dill in a round glass bowl and stir until dissolved.
2. Add the cucumbers and the onions, separated into rings in the bowl. Cover and refrigerate overnight. Keeps for a week or so. Serve with sliced tomatoes.

Minted Iced Tea

1. Boil 3 cups of water in a non-aluminum pan.
2. Add 3 heaping teaspoons of loose tea, remove from heat, cover and steep 10 minutes.
3. Strain through a cheese cloth or coffee filter into a glass pitcher.
4. Add 4 cups of cold water and 1 tablespoon of sugar, if desired.
5. Serve over ice with a sprig of mint.

A Festive Barbecue Supper

Barbecue Spareribs
Baked Cheese Grits
Coleslaw
Cornbread (see page 37)
Sweet Potato Pie

Barbecue Spareribs
   2 slabs of pork spare ribs (18" to 24" long)

Sauce
$1\frac{1}{2}$ cups cider vinegar
2 cups catsup
6 tablespoons Worcestershire sauce
2 tablespoons brown sugar
4 tablespoons butter
1 teaspoon black pepper
1 tablespoon grated onion
cayenne pepper or Tabasco to taste

1. Combine all the sauce ingredients in a saucepan and simmer for $\frac{1}{2}$ hour, stirring frequently. Let sit until ready to use.
2. Cut the ribs into two or three rib sections with kitchen shears or a knife.
3. Place in overlapping layers in a deep kettle and cover with water. Simmer, covered, for $1\frac{1}{2}$ hours, then drain.
4. Arrange in one layer in a large roasting pan lined with foil. Baste with sauce.
5. Cook the ribs in a slow oven (300 to 325 degrees) basting and turning occasionally until browned. This will take about 45 minutes.
6. Cover the pan with foil and keep warm until ready to serve. Serve with the extra sauce.

Barbecue Spareribs with Coleslaw

Baked Cheese Grits

1 cup quick grits
4 cups water
1 teaspoon salt
2 cups grated sharp yellow cheese
1 clove pressed garlic
1 stick butter
2 eggs, well beaten
$1/4$ cup milk
$1/2$ teaspoon Worcestershire sauce
$1/2$ teaspoon Tabasco, or to taste

1. Preheat the oven to 350 degrees.
2. Cook the grits in the water in a large saucepan until thick and smooth.

3. Remove from heat and add the butter and cheese, stirring until melted.
4. Stir in the garlic, salt, Tabasco, Worcestershire sauce, milk, and eggs.
5. Bake in a 1½ quart glass Pyrex casserole pan for 45 minutes to an hour, or until firm and slightly browned.

Coleslaw

1 medium head of cabbage trimmed and cut into wedges
1 green pepper, minced
1 sweet red bell pepper, minced
1 medium sweet onion minced

Dressing

½ cup sugar
1 teaspoon salt
1 teaspoon celery seed
1 teaspoon dry mustard
1 cup cider vinegar
⅔ cup vegetable oil

1. Mix the dressing ingredients in a saucepan and simmer until ready to use.
2. Chop the cabbage very fine and combine in a large bowl with onion and pepper.
3. Pour the hot sauce over mix and let sit until room temperature then refrigerate until ready to serve. Keeps well.

Sweet Potato Pie

1 prepared pastry pie crust
1 stick butter at room temperature
1 cup brown sugar
½ teaspoon of spices, combining ginger, cloves, nutmeg, allspice, and cinnamon
3 medium sweet potatoes
3 beaten eggs
¼ teaspoon salt
1 cup half and half

1. Preheat the oven to 350 degrees
2. Bake or boil the potatoes. Cool, peel, and mash. There should be about 3 cups.
3. In a mixing bowl, cream together the brown sugar and butter.
4. Mix well with the eggs.
5. Add the spices, potatoes, and half and half, mixing until well blended.
6. Pour into pie shell and bake for an hour or until set.
7. Serve with whipped cream, if desired.

Glossary

Here are some cooking terms that may need a little explanation.

Baste	To coat with pan juices or marinade using a brush made for this purpose.
Brown	To cook until a light golden brown color.
Chill	To put in the refrigerator until cool.
Chop	To cut into pieces about ½" thick.
Core	To cut the seeds, stem, and core out of a fruit.
Cream	To blend together using a spoon until the mixture reaches a creamy or smooth consistency.
Dress	To add dressing to a salad and toss lightly.
Drizzle	To pour over a few drops at a time.
Garnish	To decorate before serving.
Grease	To lightly coat with oil, margarine, or butter.
Half and Half	A product which is a combination of half milk and half cream.
Mince	Chopped into very tiny pieces.
Parboil	To plunge food into boiling water for a few minutes.
Pinch	A small amount taken between the thumb and forefinger.
Sauté	To cook quickly in butter or oil, stirring constantly.
Sift	To lighten and separate flour or other dry ingredients using a sifter.
Simmer	To cook over low heat; not boiling.
Shortening	Butter, margarine, lard, or Crisco-type product.

Index

Africa/Africans   6, 10, 12, 14, 21, 27, 32, 33
American Indians/Native Americans   10, 11, 12, 14, 19, 20, 22, 26, 27, 30, 32
Atlanta   7, 9-10

Barbecue   31-32

Charleston   9, 12, 17, 21, 30
Civil War   6, 7, 12, 22, 24
Climate   19
Colonists/Europeans   6, 10, 11, 12, 14, 17, 20, 21, 22, 27, 30, 32
Confederate States of America   6
Crops   12, 17, 19, 21, 22-23, 27

Fairs and Festivals   15-18
Farming   6, 19, 20, 21, 22, 24
Foods   12, 19, 20, 21, 23, 24, 26, 27, 28, 29, 30, 32, 33

Geography   7-9
Georgia   7, 8, 9, 10, 16, 17, 20, 22, 23, 27, 30

Jamestown   9, 11, 12-13, 22

North Carolina   6, 7, 8, 9, 10, 14, 15, 16, 18, 19, 21, 30

Plantations   12, 22, 29-30, 31, 32
Population   9-10

Recipes   34-45
  Baked Cheese Grits   43-44
  Barbecue Spareribs   42-43
  Buttermilk Biscuits   34-35
  Coleslaw   44
  Corn Pudding   39-40
  Crab Chowder   36-37
  Cucumber and Onions with Sliced Tomatoes   40-41
  Fried Ham and Apples   34-35
  Green Beans   39
  Minted Iced Tea   41
  Oven Fried Chicken   38
  Skillet Cornbread   37
  Sweet Potato Pie   45
Richmond   7

Savannah   9
Slaves/Slavery   6, 10, 12, 14, 21, 30, 32
Soul Food   32-33
South Carolina   6, 7, 8, 9, 10, 12, 14, 17, 30

Virginia   6, 7, 8, 9, 10, 11, 12, 17, 18, 19, 27, 29, 30, 31, 32

Williamsburg   9